JN232558

Kitchen Table Talk

~Anything and Everything Essays
on America and Japan~

Kitchen Table Talk
~Anything and Everything Essays on America and Japan~

Copyright © 2003 Kay Hetherly
ISBN 978-4-14-035063-8 C0082
All rights reserved.
Printed in Japan.

NHK Publishing Co., Ltd. (NHK Shuppan)
http://www.nhk-book.co.jp

No part of this book may be used or reproduced in any manner whatsoever without written permission, except in the case of brief quotations embodied in critical articles and reviews. For information, write to NHK Publishing (NHK Shuppan), 41-1 Udagawa-cho, Shibuya, Tokyo, 150-8081.

Book design by Takeshi Hatanaka
Illustrations by Rumi Nishigori
Proofreading by Mariko Kakehi

PREFACE
Kitchen Magic

Magic happens in the kitchen. And I'm not just talking about the delicious things that come from the oven. A kitchen's atmosphere is naturally warm and intimate, and talking somehow comes easier there. Any topic is possible around the kitchen table. That's the ideal I had in mind as I wrote these "anything and everything" essays for *Kitchen Table Talk*. It's an ideal that's been around for a long time in the American imagination.

In fact, many Americans will tell you that the kitchen is the "heart of the home." Surely the connection between love and cooking is strong in any culture. But the American kitchen has traditionally been a place where people gather to talk as well as to cook. In a recent memoir, *The Kitchen Congregation*,

Nora Seton writes in great detail about the central role of the kitchen in her family. "It's important not to confuse kitchens with food," she writes. The final dish is less important than the process, what she calls the "choreography of connection." This includes the way ingredients of a recipe are lovingly put together and also the way the kitchen naturally draws people in. For Seton, the kitchen was the place where she learned about life, particularly from watching and talking with her mother. It was also a place where family and friends often wandered in for long chats over coffee. Even after her mother's death, Seton writes, "When I miss my mother, I miss her in the kitchen."

But all this may sound very old-fashioned and even sexist to some people. After all, the well-known expression "a woman's place is in the home" is not what most women want to hear these days. Those words suggest that the home, particularly the kitchen, is a woman's only proper place. Of course, that's not what Seton is saying. She celebrates the power of the kitchen to connect people. She herself studied at Harvard and married a man who also loves to cook. "Men have always belonged in the kitchen," her husband tells everyone. In fact, some of my own best kitchen memories are of my father cooking huge pots of his famous vegetable soup or his spicy cheese grits. The kitchen was always filled with talk and laughter on those days. And great smells of course.

Japanese kitchens may be smaller than the average American kitchen, but magic happens there too. I used to think it was impossible to cook in my tiny Tokyo kitchen. "No place to prepare," I always complained. Then I visited friends in Gunma. Of course country kitchens are bigger than most city ones, but this kitchen was so full of pots and pans and various dishes that there seemed to be absolutely no preparation space. But that didn't stop *okaasan*. She got right down on the floor, spread out the newspaper, and started making *omanju* from scratch. Before I knew it, I was on the floor beside her, chatting and making my own funny shaped *omanju*. I have to say, they were the most delicious I have ever eaten. What made them so delicious was not simply the taste, of course, but the pleasure of making them together and being so warmly welcomed into that kitchen.

For me, these essays are kind of like that *omanju*. Each one comes from the precious experience of living in Japan, from any and every kind of conversation or encounter with people I meet and know here. Kitchen table talk, after all, is not something you can make alone. Please join me at the table!

Kay Hetherly

Contents

Polite or Not?   *10*

Saki and Sake: It Grows on You   *14*

Life's Surprises   *18*

How Do You Spell It?   *22*

I'm in a Bad Mood!   *26*

What's in a Name?   *30*

Peace Flag   *34*

Community Spirit   *38*

Some Conversational Do's and Don'ts   *43*

What's Good About a Rush-hour Train?   *47*

Everyday Heroes   *51*

The "Perfect" Meal   *55*

Church Weddings in Japan?!   *59*

Doing Things the "Right" Way   *63*

The Other Side of American Universities   *67*

No News is Good News?   *71*

The Language of Love   *75*

To Smoke or Not to Smoke   *79*

Sake and Other Things of the Heart   *83*

Body Language   *88*

The Chopsticks Debate   *93*

In Praise of Japanese Men   *97*

The Kindness of Strangers   *102*

Polite or Not?

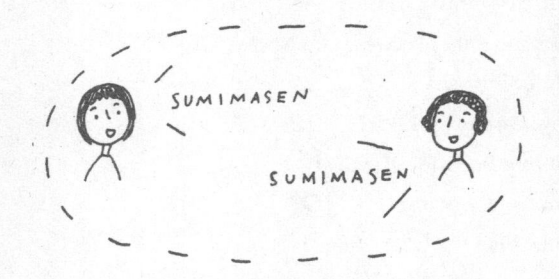

Everybody knows Japan as one of the most polite countries in the world. And foreigners who visit or live here often praise this aspect of the culture. But sometimes "politeness" is not so simple. In fact, what one person considers polite, another may consider rude or unpleasant.

I was especially surprised by the reaction of one Japanese friend, a young man in his late 20's. "Japanese people apologize too much," he complained. He was tired of hearing words like *sumimasen* and *shitsurei shimashita* all the time. As someone who often travels in Europe and America, he felt the frequent use of these kinds of words to be a strange and negative custom unique to Japan. Actually, he's right in saying that Japanese tend to apologize more than Westerners. But whether this is good or bad, of course, is a matter of personal opinion.

I myself consider this kind of politeness to be one of the most positive things about Japan. I'm often impressed by the power of the word *sumimasen*. Again and again, I've seen how using this word at just the right moment can change negative feelings into positive ones. Here's one example: I accidentally bump into a woman in a crowded station and she drops her ticket. Even though it's my fault, she apologizes first, or we both say, "*sumimasen*" at the same time. This kind of thing happens a lot, and now, having learned this custom in Japan, I try to apologize myself, even if it's the other person's fault. Such a simple idea, but it can save both people from bad feelings that might last all day.

My well-traveled friend would be right to point out that this probably wouldn't happen in America. The person at fault might say, "I'm sorry," and the other person, if they're in a good mood, may answer, "No problem," or "Don't worry about it." But it's also likely that angry words will be exchanged, especially if there's no apology from the person at fault. Something like, "Hey, watch where you're going," or perhaps even worse. The amazing thing about both people apologizing is that it almost guarantees that neither one will have bad feelings. That, I think, is very powerful.

On the other hand, sometimes what's considered very polite in Japan seems rude to me. I'm thinking specifically about the use of polite language or *keigo*, especially on the telephone. I don't dislike *keigo*, but the fact is this kind of polite language is much more difficult to understand than ordinary Japanese, especially for a foreigner. So when I call a business on the telephone to get information, the most difficult person to communicate with is usually the receptionist who answers the phone. I sometimes explain in Japanese, "Sorry, your Japanese is a little hard to understand, so could you please just use plain language?" But even if I say this, people in some service jobs seem to be trained so strictly that it's impossible for them to change their way of speaking, even for the customer's sake. I usually end up getting frustrated and sometimes even say something rude. Then I feel bad all day and they probably do too.

Politeness, I suppose, is truly polite only when it helps people to feel good or smoothes over a situation. NOT saying "*sumimasen*" if it makes someone uncomfortable, or NOT using polite language when someone doesn't understand it turns out to be the kind thing to do. There may be too much "politeness" for some people, but there's never too much kindness. ■

Saki and Sake: It Grows on You

I still remember the first time I tasted Japanese sake. It was just before moving to Kyoto from the States, and I suppose I was getting in the mood for my soon-to-come Japanese life. The liquor store had only two kinds of "saki," as Americans call it, but of course I didn't know the difference. I just bought the one with the prettiest label and invited friends over for a going away dinner. Everyone had basically the same reaction: What an odd flavor! Not bad, but not good. Just different. I never would have guessed that *nihonshu* would become one of my passions in Japan.

Of course I'm not alone. Often when I

go out, *izakaya* masters tell me that many of their foreign customers seem to love sake. In fact the person I've learned the most from is an American who's well-known as an expert: John Gauntner has written books, created internet web sites, and had a monthly *nihonshu* column in the *Japan Times* for many years. He also holds regular sake evenings at pubs in Tokyo. These evenings include short lectures about *nihonshu* in English and the opportunity to try a variety of sake with a nice meal. It's also a great chance to meet and talk with other sake lovers.

Recently I attended one of these evenings for the first time. The main event was a "blind tasting" of eight different *junmai* sakes from eight different prefectures. All the unlabeled bottles were numbered and put on a big table. Then the thirty or so participants slowly went from bottle to bottle, smelling, tasting, taking notes, and finally ranking each one. When everyone was finished, we sat down and, while eating and drinking together, learned the results.

If this sounds like serious business, it wasn't. Most of the participants, which included a lot of Americans, a few Japanese, and at least one German, were like me — not experts, but just people who love good sake. We were like kids turned loose in a candy store! Of course there was the pleasure of tasting and ranking eight high quality sakes, but it was the atmosphere that really made it fun. Lots of laughing and joking as we moved around the table, and then the excitement of hearing the results and cheering for our favorites.

The results were fascinating. Although there was one clear favorite which got seventeen votes (including mine) as number one, the rest of the votes were divided fairly evenly among each of the other seven choices. In fact, the sake I liked the least was another person's favorite. Not only that, but while one of my favorites seemed "fruity and sweet" to me, another person said it tasted like "tar." And this is exactly what makes *nihonshu* so interesting. The taste is complex and very personal. In fact the very same sake never seems to taste exactly the same way twice.

I suppose it's natural for *nihonshu* to be popular in Japan among non-Japanese as well as natives. It just goes with the food here and with the atmosphere of Japanese pubs. But, according to a recent article, even in New York "sake bars" are becoming popular. That doesn't surprise me. Though sake may taste a little odd at first, it's a taste that grows on you; in other words, it's something you come to like more and more with time. That has certainly been true for me. I've come a long way from my first encounter with "saki," and it just gets better and better. ∎

Life's Surprises

The party starts at 7:00!

I wish I had kept a diary when I first moved to Japan. Every day was such an adventure, full of surprises. I've forgotten a lot of the small things that delighted me then, but I'll never forget the first party I gave.

I was teaching English at Ritsumeikan University in Kyoto with several other American and English teachers. We decided to have a party for some of our students at my apartment which was close to the school. The party was at 7:00. As usual, I was rushing to get ready, cleaning the apartment, checking the food, and finally at about 6:45, I was about to take a quick shower and get dressed. Perfect timing, I thought. But just then, the doorbell rang. The students, in one big group, were already at my door!

Now, I admit that waiting until 6:45 to get in the shower is cutting things pretty close. But if it were an American party, there would be no problem. Nobody comes early, and in fact, most people come a little late on purpose, usually alone or in pairs. We call it being "fashionably late." So if my students had followed the American custom, I would have been ready for them when they came. But I wasn't, and I had to ask them to wait outside for about 15 minutes. "The party starts at 7:00!" I scolded. This was a real life lesson for them and for me about cultural differences. They learned never to come to my parties early again, and I learned to be ready a little early just in case.

So at 7:00, everyone came in, along with my second surprise. They showered me with all kinds of presents! I was pleased, of course, but that's when I really wished they hadn't all come together. I was so busy finding vases for the flowers, bowls for the snacks, and trying to thank everyone properly for their gifts, it was impossible to serve anyone. It's not unusual to take something like a bottle of wine to an American-style party, but I had never felt so appreciated (and overwhelmed) by my guests before. It seemed more like my birthday or Christmas than a simple home party.

I did finally manage to serve them all though, we had our *kanpai*, and everyone seemed to be having a good time. Then came my next, and most embarrassing, surprise. One student came out of the bathroom, and said to me, in front of everyone, "Why do you have that pink thing in the bathroom? That's supposed to go in the closet to protect your clothes from bugs." Not being able to read Japanese, I had thought it was an air freshener for the bathroom. We all had a good laugh, and I got a shopping lesson from my students.

Sometimes I'm still surprised by things

in Japan, but the funny thing is, now the biggest surprises often come when I go back to visit the US. Last time I was there, I saw something I can't imagine seeing in Japan. While driving down a country road, I noticed a woman up ahead, jogging on the side of the road and pushing something in front of her. As I got closer, I realized she was pushing a baby carriage, and her baby was inside. It was a special carriage made for joggers with babies. It's true that a lot of American mothers refuse to give up their own interests for the sake of their babies, but I had never seen anything like this before.

Life is certainly full of surprises, no matter where you are. ∎

How Do You Spell It?

in my dairy life

"I am not a key!" Sometimes I tell my students this while waving my keys around dramatically, hoping they'll remember. Some do, but some will inevitably keep writing my name as Key, not Kay, all through the semester. I'm used to this, and though it doesn't especially bother me, it does make me wonder about Japanese attitudes toward spelling English words.

I'm the first to admit how difficult English spelling is, and *katakana* doesn't make it any easier. There's no doubt about that. I also admit that sometimes I enjoy the mistakes that students make. I laugh every time someone writes "in my dairy life" instead of "daily life." I always imagine the writer getting up early to milk the cows and clean the barn. Another favorite is "Please give her a massage" rather than "a message." If we gave a massage every time we were supposed to give a message, there would be a lot fewer people around with stiff backs and shoulders.

But seriously, I do sometimes wonder whether spelling is considered important or not in the English language classroom in Japan. When I was an elementary school student, spelling was one of my favorite subjects. We had spelling tests and spelling bees (contests) every week. Believe it or not, I can still remember the feel of the pages and the smell of my old spelling textbook. Back then, we were taught that good spelling was essential for good writing. And that same lesson was taught all the way through college and even afterwards. For example, I was always told, if you make spelling mistakes on your resume or cover letter, don't expect to get the job. In other words, your writing, which includes spelling, makes a strong first impression and says something about your character and reliability.

I imagine the same thing is true about written Japanese. Writing the wrong *kanji* or writing the right one incorrectly would probably not make a good impression and might even keep you from getting into a certain school or company.

But if that's true, if Japanese share that same value in their own language, why are English words so often misspelled in Japan? The most obvious example is in business and advertising, and sometimes the mistake is very dramatic. Anyone who knows or likes English has probably noticed this. You'll see a big sign on a hotel that reads "Liver Hotel" instead of "River Hotel." Is this a hotel for recovering alcoholics (give your liver a rest!)? Of course it makes us laugh, but on another level it is sloppy English.

In fact, this was an actual example that came up in a recent discussion among writers and editors of English working in Japan. People were asking, how can this happen? If a company spends a lot of money to create a slogan or a big sign in English, why don't they at least make sure it's correct first? Some people suggested that English used in Japanese advertising is simply decoration. It's written for Japanese people, not native English speakers, so as long as the message gets across, nobody cares whether it's "good" English or not.

Maybe it's true that most Japanese don't even think of these signs and slogans as real English. But I still worry about the influence this kind of public sloppiness might have on how people learn English in Japan. If Japanese are constantly surrounded by images of strange English, they may, perhaps unconsciously, start to believe that spelling and accuracy really don't matter. But, in fact, at least in the real English world, they definitely do. ∎

I'm in a Bad Mood!

The other day, I met an American colleague in the elevator. We hadn't seen each other for awhile, but he didn't say, "Hi Kay," or "How have you been?" Rather, the first thing he said to me was, "I'm in a bad mood. It's been a terrible day!" I was a little surprised—but only for a second. No one in Japan had ever greeted me this way before. But I actually found something refreshing in his honesty.

Soon after that, I happened to be watching Woody Allen's classic film, *Annie Hall*. There's a hilarious scene where Annie gets out of a taxi in New York, and her boyfriend, Alvy, is waiting for her. He's upset that she's late, but the first thing she says is, "I'm in a bad mood. OK?" As if that explains everything. But it doesn't. He's in a bad mood too, so they end up having a long and loud argument in front of the movie theater.

The scene is very funny, but this kind of American "noisiness" in real life usually makes me uncomfortable. I especially dislike the way people tend to interrupt each other when talking or arguing. In fact, I've often thought that, in general, Japanese are much better listeners than Americans. But I have to admit there's something liberating about being able to say, "I'm in a bad mood" and then spill out what's bothering you. The key though is that the person you're talking to has to be willing to listen.

That's the point, I think. People usually say "I'm in a bad mood," because they want a sympathetic ear. If they can express their troubles freely to someone, it makes them feel better. They get the problem "off their chest" as we say in English.

In fact, though I had forgotten until my encounter in the elevator, Americans often start a conversation like this. I've done it myself. But I had never greeted a Japanese friend in the same way. So one day I decided to try it.

I was supposed to meet my friend at 6:30. Usually I ride my bike, but it was cold and rainy so I decided to take a taxi. Of course all the taxis were full. Then when I finally saw an empty one, someone stepped out right in front of me and took it. This happened twice! It was getting late and there were no more taxis in sight. So I went home, got my bike, and rode the cold, miserable ten minutes to the station. By then, I was about fifteen minutes late and in a terrible mood. Ordinarily, I would get control of myself, try to forget my bad feeling, meet my friend, and have a nice evening.

But this time I decided to just say how I felt: "I'm in a bad mood. I want to kill someone!" Half-laughing, this is how I greeted my poor friend in Japanese. Later someone told me no one would ever say this because the language is too shocking. Of course I didn't mean it literally. But in English we often exaggerate like this to express strong emotion, and it made me feel better to say it. Fortunately, my friend was kind enough to listen to my troubles, and then we had a good laugh about my bad mood and my inappropriate Japanese.

I'm not recommending this kind of greeting. Most people would agree it's much nicer to be cheerful when we meet someone. But the fact is sometimes we are in bad mood and it's a relief to be able to just say it. And if you're lucky enough to have a friend who'll listen and let you get it off your chest, that's probably enough to put you back in a pretty good mood after all. ∎

What's in a Name?

When I asked my freshmen students to explain their Japanese names in English, some of them seemed to think I was crazy. In fact, many said their names had no meaning. This surprised me because I often hear Japanese people explaining the kanji in their names when they introduce themselves for the first time. And for Westerners, this aspect of *kanji* can be fascinating, especially considering most Western names have no special image or meaning.

Some students, though, did have interesting stories about their names. They explained how their parents carefully chose each character in their first name to express some kind of hope or expectation for them. Or they talked about the connection of their last name with a particular region of Japan. Most of these students seemed to be proud of their names and also happy to have this kind of family story to tell. I suspect many of them will continue the tradition of choosing special first names for their own children.

Of course, American parents also think hard about what to name their children. Some English names do have a specific meaning or at least an image. For example the names "March," "April," "May," and "June," which are all girls' names, come from the months of spring and early summer and may suggest beauty, hope, or the beginning of things. For boys, names like "Butch" and "Spike" have a tough, strong image.

But these kinds of names are actually pretty rare. It's more common for parents to simply choose a name they like, perhaps one that's currently in fashion, like the name of a TV character or public figure. Names in the family are also popular, for example, naming a daughter after her grandmother or a son after a favorite brother. Using names from the Bible or other famous books is common too. One of my girlfriends was named "Beth" and her little sister, "Meg," after the girls in the popular book *Little Women*. In my own family, each person has a first name of only three letters.

Anyone who has read books or seen movies about the American South may have noticed something interesting about Southern names. Although most Americans have a first, middle, and last name, middle names really aren't used much. But in the South, quite a lot of people are called by their first and middle name, as one name. "Billy Bob" (like the famous film director/actor Billy Bob Thornton), is a typical one for guys. Middle names are often used for scolding as well! I was always called "Kay" or "Katy" by my parents except when I was in trouble. Then suddenly I became "Kay Lynn." Maybe that's why I don't like to use my middle name now.

But whether we like or dislike our names, they are an intimate part of our identity. Unlike most things, we keep them our whole lives, and there's a kind of comfort in that. It's not surprising then that some women prefer to keep their original name when they get married rather than taking their husband's last name. It's not only an expression of equality, but also a way of not losing one's separate identity within the marriage. At least some women think so.

Names are, after all, who we are. They may reflect our parents' hopes for us or remind us of where we came from. I've always thought Japanese were lucky to have kanji for naming. With all its beauty and variety, I can't imagine a better way to express something so personal as a name. ∎

Peace Flag

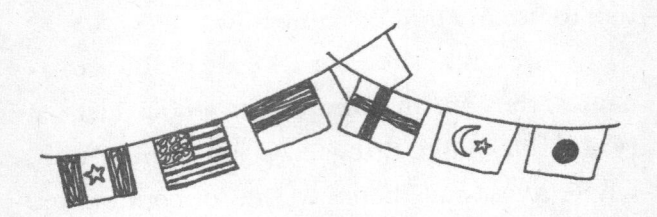

Almost one year has passed since the event known all over the world as September 11th, or just 9/11. In a year's time, though some wounds have surely healed, America and the world are still scarred by the images of those airplanes crashing through the middle of the World Trade Center in the heart of New York. While there are still many difficult and controversial issues surrounding the attack and what happened after it, I'd like to consider what seems to me a simple idea, something I thought about many times in the weeks and months after September 11th.

Like so many other people, I was especially moved by the way Americans came together after the attack. Even New Yorkers, typically known for their fast pace and big city unfriendliness, slowed down and reached out to each other. People all over the country said they felt connected in ways they had never felt before. At that time, all you had to do was turn on the TV news to see images of people, often strangers, gathering together to sing, pray, grieve, or just feel their togetherness. This is something Americans really seemed to need at that time. It was part of the healing process, the effort to return to a normal life. Many people recognized that in the midst of this terrible national tragedy, something beautiful had been born.

People also showed their togetherness with the American flag. Even among my own friends, some who had never owned or wanted a flag before went out and bought one or more. I, and the world perhaps, saw more American flags in those months after the attack than ever before. But while it's easy to understand the emotion behind wanting to wave the flag along with the rest of the country, the flag-waving itself really bothered me during the days following 9/11.

Who knows? If I had been living in America at this time last year, maybe I would have done the same thing. But somehow, from a distance, the American flag looks different. It does not represent only the simple, pure feeling of loving your country and its people. The flag is a symbol which many people, particularly non-Americans, associate with things like nationalism, arrogance, power, and war. Intentionally or not, waving the flag as a whole country sends a message to the world and to the American President that the entire country is behind him and whatever he wants to do. Of course, it is true that the majority of Americans did support the President's actions. But not everyone who waved the flag wanted war. The media emphasized the unity of the country and support for the President, but behind the scenes, peace rallies and calls for a different solution were not uncommon.

Which leads me, finally, to my simple (maybe too simple?) idea. The world needs a powerful peace flag. Or maybe each country needs its own peace flag. This flag could symbolize love for a country and its people, or love for humanity, and the desire for world peace. Waving this flag would represent a demand for action, not simply a dreamy idea of peace. But the action would have to be some solution other than war.

I don't know if waving a peace flag rather than the heavily symbolic American flag would have made a difference in what happened after September 11th. But I do believe that if Americans had had a choice, we would have seen many peace flags flying. And perhaps people all over the world would have joined in and shown that we are, after all, one human family. ■

Community Spirit

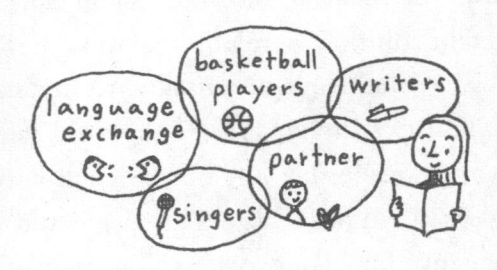

It might surprise a lot of people in Japan to know how large and active the international English-speaking community here is. Actually I'm surprised myself. Since I came to Japan hoping to immerse myself in the culture and language of this country as much as possible, I suppose I've avoided spending too much time with other Westerners. Recently though I've learned more about what Westerners are doing around Japan, and I've realized just how impressive this community is.

Thanks to one woman in particular, Caroline Pover from the UK, I've become aware of an amazing support system for

Western women living in Japan. In 2001, Pover published a book called *Being a Broad in Japan: Everything a Western Woman Needs to Survive and Thrive.* She has collected information on how to do just about anything in Japan as a foreigner, from running a business to dating Japanese men. Her book is filled with facts, statistics, and contact information for almost every need. But she also includes interviews with hundreds of women who speak frankly about their experiences of living and working in Japan. So while the book is an encyclopedia of useful information, it's also a fascinating read for anyone interested in how Western women see and experience Japan.

What's more, Pover introduces a list of women's organizations based in Japan for both professionals and non-professionals. Most welcome Japanese members and many are also open to men. One group, Digital Eve Japan, is especially for women who want to share knowledge about computers. This group supports women of all nationalities through an e-mail discussion list and website, and through actual workshops and parties where members can meet to get hands-on computer experience and learn about job possibilities in Japan. In fact, many organizations listed in the book offer this kind of online and offline support, often providing valuable job connections for those who want to work in a bilingual environment.

Not surprisingly, one of the most interesting of these organizations is the one Pover herself started. Like the book, it was designed mainly to support foreign women living in Japan, though Japanese members are also welcome. On an internet discussion board, members share daily experiences of living abroad and give each other practical and sometimes very personal advice. "Where's the best place to have a baby in Japan?" "Do I really need to buy a *hanko*?" "I'm homesick and lonely. How can I make friends here?" These are just a few topics that have come up recently. Members often write long, detailed comments to help each other out, though most have never even met. It's comforting to know that this community is always there, happy to help or just chat if that's what you need.

Internet communities are nice because you can participate in the conversation no matter where you live. But internet groups are only the tip of the international community in Japan. In Tokyo, for example, whatever your interest is, you can find a group that will welcome you. Just look in *Metropolis*, Tokyo's free weekly English magazine, and you'll find clubs for runners, basketball players, writers, businesspeople, book lovers, and the list goes on. You can also find a language exchange partner or even a date!

Of course it's wonderful for foreigners to have so many resources to support their lives in Japan. At the same time, these groups also offer Japanese and non-Japanese a valuable chance to communicate, meet each other, and even work together. The resources and the community spirit are out there. It's just up to each of us to choose what's best and open our world a little wider. ∎

Some Conversational Do's and Don'ts

At one time or another, many Japanese find themselves face to face with a foreigner that they're meeting for the first time. It may be at some kind of party, at the local sports club, or possibly sitting together on a long airplane trip. Of course some people feel comfortable in this situation, but others may wonder what they should talk about. I'd like to suggest a few do's and don'ts for making conversation with a foreigner that, hopefully, will be satisfying for both of you. Of course these are only my personal suggestions, so don't take them too seriously, and don't be surprised if another foreigner living in Japan has a different opinion!

First of all, do find out how long the person has lived in Japan. If they're a tourist or someone who's been here a short time, say a year or less, then making conversation should be pretty simple. They'll probably enjoy talking about their impressions of Japan, Japanese food, why they came, and what they plan to do while they're here. In other words, they won't mind being treated like a guest or a visitor if that's what they are. And it's likely that they'll really appreciate your ability to speak to them in English or simple Japanese. People who spend a fairly short time in Japan almost always talk with great fondness about the kindness of the Japanese people they've met. I think this is because most Japanese are good at this kind of conversation and sincere in wanting to welcome people from other countries to Japan.

It's the long term residents in Japan that present more of a conversational challenge, I believe. The longer a person has been in a foreign country, the more they want to fit in and forget as much as possible that they're a foreigner. After all, words like *gaijin* and *foreigner* basically mean "outsider." And nobody really wants to be an outsider. So do try to see them as one of the group rather than as someone different and special. In other words, don't focus too much on topics that set them apart, like how well they use chopsticks, their ability to eat sashimi, or how different their physical characteristics are. And don't ask them to practice English with you!

In fact, a good question to ask yourself is what do you talk about with your Japanese friends when you go out? Just keep in mind that the resident foreigners you meet would probably enjoy the same kind of conversation. Some things I like talking about with new or old friends are sports, books, movies, *nihonshu*, food, TV dramas, interesting things in the news, and sometimes more personal topics as well.

The other day I happened to meet one of my colleagues on the bus, and this was our first chance to have a real conversation together. Like a lot of people, I'm not so interested in talking about work when I'm not working. So I asked him what he likes to do for fun. He started talking about fishing, and this led to a wonderful story about the man who taught him how to fish when he was a boy. After our 20 minute or so conversation, I felt great. He had told me a moving personal story, we had discovered a common interest — fishing — and I had completely forgotten that I was a "foreigner."

For me, a satisfying conversation is one of life's greatest pleasures. I look forward to many many more while I'm in Japan and wish the same for all of you. ■

What's Good About a Rush-hour Train?

"NOTHING!" This seems like the most appropriate answer to the question, "What's good about a rush-hour train?" Just about everyone, inside and outside of Japan, has seen or heard about station workers pushing people onto crowded Tokyo trains. Just when you think it's impossible for even one more person to get on, three, four, or even five more people are pushed in, right as the doors are closing. Forget about trying to read your book, or even move your arm! What could possibly be good about this?

For some strange reason, though, crowded Tokyo trains have never bothered me much. But then, I've been fairly lucky until recently. Though I did have to commute to work for over an hour, I usually didn't have to do it during rush hour. That changed when I went back to school for a year. Suddenly I found myself on the rush-hour train every morning. Of course it can be very unpleasant to be crammed into such a small space with so many people. But most of the time, I feel quite philosophical about it all.

When you think about it, human beings are truly amazing. We can get used to almost any situation if we have to. When I look around me at all those people on the train, I often feel a great fondness for humanity. Nobody wants to be crowded into such a small space, but there we are, and we make the best of it. Nobody yells, nobody fights, nobody even gives anyone a dirty look. We may be thinking bad thoughts about the person whose elbow is sticking into our back, or the person breathing right into our ear, but most people seem to make a real effort not to cause any trouble. Of course there is the occasional groper or weirdo who tries to take advantage of the situation, but they are clearly the exception. Basically the feeling is, "Hey, we're all in this together and we'll get through it somehow. It's only temporary." At least that's the way it seems to me.

It's hard to imagine this kind of rush-hour train in America. Most Americans probably wouldn't put up with being packed together with so many people every morning and evening. Surely angry words would be spoken. Fights would break out. But that's a good thing, many people would say. No one should put up with that kind of crowding. In Japan, though, at least in Tokyo, most people have to ride the trains in order to get to work or school on time. The kind of car culture that has developed in a lot of big American cities would be impossible here. There's simply not enough space. It is a luxury to be able to drive to work in the privacy of your own car, but that's not a simple solution either. In most big American cities outside of the Northeast, there are no commuter trains or subways, and almost everyone drives to work. Traffic is terrible, and people often end up sitting in their cars for hours in traffic jams. If there's an accident, which is common, it takes even longer. There tends to be a lot of honking of horns and even occasional "road rage" when people lose their temper from not being able to move faster.

It's certainly not a perfect world when we have to choose between crowded trains or crowded roads. But being in a traffic jam never made me feel the togetherness of people the way I often feel it on Tokyo trains. And for me, that's what's good about rush-hour trains. ■

Everyday Heroes

Every American kid wants to be a hero. We grow up on a heavy diet of Superman, Batman, and cowboy movies, where the good guy always beats up the bad guy. Or Tarzan movies, where Tarzan always saves Jane just as she's about to be eaten by some wild animal. Even as a girl, I imagined myself to be Tarzan, not Jane. Of course, if I were in trouble, I wouldn't mind being saved by a strong, brave man. Still, I'd really rather be the hero myself. Maybe not all American girls feel this way, but I do think it would be hard to grow up as a boy in America and not want to be a hero. It seems to be built so deeply into the culture that even after growing up, most people would still love the chance to be called a "hero."

I wonder how many Japanese kids and adults feel the same way. Surely super-hero stories are popular here just as they are in the US. But the other day I saw a scene in a TV drama that made me wonder about this. It was a scene I couldn't imagine seeing on American TV.

Here's the situation: A businessman is out walking with an attractive younger woman. She's clearly interested in him, and this is their first "date." The scene takes place at night somewhere in Tokyo where lots of people are walking around. Suddenly the two notice a fight on a dark street. Some young boys are attacking a helpless older man. The businessman stops and watches, but he doesn't say or do anything. His date wants him to ignore the fight and get away as fast as possible, but he stands there watching. Finally the boys see him and start attacking him too. The woman calls for help to people walking by, but no one stops. In the end, the boys leave, and the businessman is ok, but the relationship between him and young woman is over. They never go out together again.

What shocked me the most about this scene was the woman's reaction. First, she begs the man to run away, and then she's ashamed when he gets involved. If this were an American drama, the woman would have said to her date, "Quick! Do something!" She would have expected him to try to be a hero and save the old man. And even if he failed, she would have admired him for trying. On the other hand, if he ran away from the scene, doing nothing to help, that would surely be the end of the relationship. The woman would probably never go out with him again.

This kind of situation is not only in TV dramas of course. We sometimes hear similar stories on the news. Many of us have personal stories as well about ignoring some incident, like groping, or about being ignored ourselves when we needed help. In fact, it seems to be generally accepted, at least in Tokyo, that not getting involved is the smart thing to do. That does make sense in a way. Getting involved can be dangerous. In fact, you might even make the situation worse than it already is. It's especially easy to feel that way when you live in a big city where you may not even know your own neighbors. But the fact is the victim could very easily be your neighbor. Or you. Or someone you love. And that's when you may really hope that somebody in the crowd will at least try to be a hero. ∎

The "Perfect" Meal

Some Americans celebrate eating every day, but there are two days during the year when the whole country celebrates mealtime together: Thanksgiving and Christmas. It's natural on these two special days for cooks to try and create the "perfect" meal. Americans who live abroad are no different. Many of us try to keep up our family holiday traditions even though there may be mostly friends, rather than family, around the dinner table.

I'll never forget my first Thanksgiving dinner in Japan. I was determined to make exactly the same kind of meal that I would have made at home in Texas. I was so relieved to find all the ingredients I needed, even a turkey, at either the local grocery store or the international market. After that, all I had to do was make those holiday dishes I had made so many times before. Nothing to it! Or so I thought.

At serving time, I realized how difficult it is to have a truly American-style Thanksgiving in Japan. Traditionally, serving time is when Mom, with everyone's help, miraculously gets everything from the stove onto the table piping hot. Then, as Dad carves the turkey, warm from the oven, all the dishes are passed around and everyone takes a helping of each one. Finally when everyone is served, the meal starts. For a "perfect" meal, those two points can't be ignored: First, other than salads, everything has to be hot. And second, everyone starts and ends together. When I cooked my first few holiday dinners in Japan, it was these two points that got me into trouble.

Getting everything onto the table when it's still hot is quite a challenge, even if you have the typical 4-burner American stove. But with only 2 burners, as most Japanese kitchens have, it's almost impossible. On top of that, expectations are simply different. It's not even important for everything to be hot in a Japanese meal. Just think about the big New Year's Day meal here. Most foods are served cold or at room temperature. Another difference is the custom of everyone eating together, from the beginning to the end of the meal. In Japan the cook may bring dishes out of the kitchen one by one as they're made. So there's no need for everything to be hot at the same time or for everyone to be at the table together. All these differences show that what's "perfect" in a meal really depends on the customs of a particular place.

For my first few holiday meals in Japan, I didn't realize this. So I rushed around madly, trying to get the whole meal on the table while it was still hot. Meanwhile, my mostly Japanese guests had no idea why I was rushing around like that. It was chaos! Certainly not the relaxed atmosphere I had hoped to create. Years later though, I talked to an English friend in Japan who had exactly the same experience. Like an American meal, the "perfect" English meal also has to be hot. My friend confessed that every Christmas meal in Japan was chaos, with her rushing around and her Japanese guests looking on in confusion.

It's taken awhile, but I finally learned a great lesson from all this: Forget perfection. Sometimes you have to let go of tradition and accept the situation as it is. The "perfect" meal, after all, has more to do with good food, good company, and a relaxing atmosphere than with serving the same way your mother did. In fact, last Christmas the cold sweet potatoes didn't even bother me. Now that's progress. ∎

Church Weddings in Japan?!

The other day the subject of weddings came up in my Japanese class. When the teacher told us that church weddings were quite fashionable in Japan these days, some of the Western students were shocked. They started asking questions like, "You mean even if the couple getting married aren't Christians?" and "Does a real priest perform the ceremony?" I could see from their faces and the tone of their questions that this seemed very, very strange to them. Then suddenly it occurred to me, hey, this is no different from America!

It's true. The majority of Americans are

married in a Christian church by a minister or priest whether they're believers or not. Some Japanese have the idea that all Americans are Christians, but this is false. Other than Christians, which includes both Catholics and Protestants, there are also Americans who are Jewish, Muslim, Buddhist, just to name a few, and plenty of people who have no religion at all. It might be impossible for a non-Catholic to be married in a Catholic church, but among Protestants, there are many different groups, some strict and some very open. Non-Christians who want a church wedding can easily find a Protestant minister to perform the ceremony — and that is just what most non-Christians choose to do. So in that case, it's really not so different from Japanese having a Christian wedding even when they're not Christians.

But why do Americans who aren't religious do it? There are other ways to get married. In fact, some people have home weddings and some even go down to the city hall and get a license from the justice of the peace with no ceremony at all. But church weddings are by far the most popular, and for some of the same reasons that they're popular in Japan: a church has a nice atmosphere and a romantic image. Of course, it's also a long tradition in Western culture. After all, the image of a wedding for most Americans is a church wedding, and some little girls dream about "the big day" long before they're old enough to marry.

But one thing has changed about American weddings since my mother's generation. A lot of couples these days write their own vows or ask the priest to change some of the words in the traditional Christian ceremony. Some couples do this to make their wedding more personal or romantic, but some do it because they consider the traditional vows old-fashioned or even sexist. In particular, the woman's words, which have been used as far back as the 14th Century in England, are to "love, honor, and obey" her husband. The problem, of course, is the word *obey*. It may surprise people with an image of America as a country where men and women are equal, but most women said these words until fairly recently, and even now some couples still choose these vows for their wedding. I suppose some choose these words because they believe in a traditional kind of marriage, with the man as head of the household, but for others, perhaps, the ritual itself is more important than the actual words that are spoken.

Either way, there's no doubt that the Christian wedding ceremony is a powerful ritual. If you think about it, it's not hard to understand why non-Christians might also be attracted to it, whether they live in Japan or America. My surprised classmates made me realize that while it's easy to notice what seems "strange" in a foreign country, we often don't see that the same "strangeness" is in our own culture as well. ∎

Doing Things the "Right" Way

One of my favorite movies has a great birthday party scene at the end. Based on a play called *Crimes of the Heart* (*Lonely Hearts* in Japan), this movie is about three sisters in Mississippi. In that last scene, they're celebrating the 30th birthday of the oldest sister, Lenny, in typical American style. The two younger sisters bring out the cake with 31 candles lit up (one to grow on!). Then, after they sing "Happy Birthday," Lenny makes a secret wish, takes a deep breath, and blows out all the candles with that one breath. Everyone cheers. When I saw this scene again recently, I felt such satisfaction and relief as I watched Lenny blow out those candles. Then I realized why. I was thinking, "Somebody did it the right way, finally!"

Of course I realize the "right" way is simply the way I've always done it myself. I suppose most of us, no matter where we come from, grow up believing our own way of doing things is right. And when someone doesn't follow our way, it bothers us. That's how I feel when I watch Japanese friends blow out birthday candles. First of all, they don't make a wish, and second, they keep blowing and blowing, taking two or three breaths, before the candles are finally out. I've even seen someone who's not the birthday person help with the blowing. And what's worse, nobody seems to notice or mind any of this, except me. In fact, I didn't even realize how much I minded until I saw the scene in that movie again and felt so happy when Lenny did it RIGHT.

It all seems a little silly when you think about it. This kind of ritual is just superstition after all. The idea is that if you blow all your candles out with one breath, your birthday wish will come true. But as long as everyone's having fun, who's to say what's right or wrong or how people should celebrate? I guess it surprised me to realize how attached I am to this kind of small ritual.

Then I started wondering about all the things I must be doing "wrong" in Japan. People don't say anything because they're polite, but there must be hundreds of social rituals and customs I don't know or don't follow. Like the way I wad up my umbrella. Both Japanese men and women crease theirs so very carefully in just the right places and fold them up perfectly. I try to be as inconspicuous as possible as I wad my own umbrella up and snap it closed, not wanting to bother with the creases, but surely some people notice. Maybe they feel disgusted, or perhaps they feel sorry for me, wondering why in the world my parents didn't teach me properly.

Come to think of it, even I find myself feeling superior when I notice another non-Japanese person messing up a perfectly good Japanese way of doing something. In fact, during my last visit to Texas, I was pleasantly surprised to find *edamame* on my friends' dinner table. But when I watched everyone eating it, I was appalled. They didn't pop the little beans into their mouths from the pod the way they were supposed to. No, they ripped the pod apart, and then ate the beans one by one with their fingers. I couldn't bear to watch.

Of course, there's always more than one way of doing things. Being different doesn't necessarily make it wrong. Now, if I can just remember that the next time I go to a birthday party in Japan... ■

The Other Side of American Universities

"Japanese universities are hard to get into and easy to graduate from, but American universities are easy to get into and hard to graduate from."

This is a statement I've heard countless times in Japan from Japanese, Americans, and most recently from a Korean friend. Like a cliche, it's repeated over and over because it has some truth to it, but it's a very superficial kind of truth that may lead to misunderstanding.

Let's start with the idea that American universities are easy to get into. It would be more accurate to say that most people with a high school education can probably find a university that will accept them somewhere in America. In other words, entrance standards are very different from university to university, just as they are in Japan. It's certainly not easy to get into the top schools like Harvard or Columbia (believe me, I tried!), but it's also not easy to get into the better schools in each state. In my home state, while some schools may be very easy to enter, the University of Texas at Austin, which is considered the best public university there, has a reputation for being quite selective.

And how about graduating? Again, it all depends on where you go. Most people in Japan know about the best American universities, the Ivy League schools, for example, or the state schools that make the top ten lists, like the University of California at Berkeley. At these and a lot of other schools, students have to work hard to do well in their classes. But one thing people may not know is that, unlike

Japanese universities, a "D" is a passing grade at most schools. Also in most undergraduate programs, students can graduate with a "C" average in their classes. That means someone who makes mainly "C's" will have a low grade point average (GPA) and may be at the bottom of their graduating class, but they can still graduate and receive a diploma, just like someone with all "A's." And in most American schools, it's not that difficult to be a "C" student.

Then there are the "party schools." Just like it sounds, a party school is a university with a reputation for good parties rather than good academics. A lot of students go there for fun, not to study. That doesn't necessarily mean they don't graduate. It just means they probably skip classes fairly often, find out who the "easy" teachers are, and have a busy social life with lots of keg parties (as in a "keg" or barrel of beer). I hate to admit it, but my undergraduate school in Texas had a reputation as a party school. There were good teachers and students there as well and some hard classes, but there was also a beautiful river running through the center of town, crowded with students who were supposed to be in class. Of course, some of them didn't graduate, but others made sure to keep their "C" average so they could.

No doubt, there are real differences between Japanese and American universities, including how students enter and graduate. But simply saying that it's easy to graduate in Japan and hard in America tends to overvalue an American university education and undervalue a Japanese one. It's also unfair to the Japanese students who do work hard and too generous to the students at American universities who graduate with very little effort. Isn't it time to throw out this kind of tired cliche and simply give credit where credit is due? ■

No News is Good News?

What are some recent stories in the news? Another political scandal. A kidnapping. More crimes by teenagers. Let's face it. Most of the news we see on TV or in newspapers is bad news. That's why some people say, "No news is good news." If the announcer appeared on TV and said, "Sorry folks, there's no news today," that would probably mean nothing bad happened. And that would be good news.

But is no news really good news? I, for one, would like to see and hear more stories about the good things that happen every day. In particular, it seems that young people in Japan get a lot of bad press — that is, the media image of Japanese youth is often negative. People who have little or no real contact or communication with young people may even believe this negative image is the whole story.

I suppose this is nothing new though. For some reason, young people are always an easy target. This is true in America as well as Japan. Adults in every generation, it seems, complain that the younger generation is going to the dogs: they're lazy or selfish; "parasite singles"; they have no manners, no direction; their test scores and intelligence are falling. I've heard these kinds of things for years. In fact, my parents' generation said the same kinds of things about us. They didn't like our clothes or our hairstyles. Our music was just noise. And we had no manners! It's natural, I suppose, to want young people to be better, but too often we miss the good things.

I've been guilty of this myself. One year I had a group of female students who dressed in the *ko-gyaru* fashion: heavy makeup, short skirts, big shoes, blond hair. I assumed they were not very smart and not very interested in school. I was wrong. As I got to know some of these girls, as I listened to their opinions and read their writing, I realized they were some of the smartest and most ambitious students I had ever had.

In fact, I am extremely lucky. As a teacher, I'm in close contact with young people every week. I learn a lot about what they're thinking and who they are. There are certainly many different personalities and opinions among them, but here are a few things I think it's safe to generalize about. Most of them are passionate about peace. War is unthinkable for them. Racism is also unforgivable for most of them. They may admit that, like most human beings, they have prejudices and stereotypes. But they are hurt and truly saddened by inequality based on race or cultural differences. They love their families, though many are struggling to get along and communicate better with parents. And finally, they are thinking very seriously about things like human relations, how to have a meaningful life, and how to make a better world.

Sure, there are plenty of young people in Japan who are lost and thinking only about themselves or their own small group. There are those who anger us with bad manners or worse. And these are the ones we usually hear about on the news or notice on the street. If this were the whole story, I would feel discouraged. But, fortunately it's not. Year after year, as I get to know more and more young people and hear what they're thinking about, I feel great hope for the future. These are the kind of young people I'd like to see more of on TV or in newspapers and magazines. And that would truly be good news. ∎

The Language of Love

I've never been a big fan of Valentine's Day, Japanese style. Do we really need a day when only women show their appreciation or affection for men? That seems to miss the whole point somehow. Valentine's Day should be for everyone.

I loved Valentine's Day as a kid. Everyone at school exchanged cards and you could find out if the boy you liked at school felt the same way about you. If he put a special message on your card, you knew. Of course, you could let him know the same way. But not only that, Valentine's Day was the day when your mother would bring home heart-shaped chocolate cakes from the bakery. That was her message of love. It seems odd that we need a special day for showing love or affection. But the truth is, most people tend to forget or just don't take the time to do it in their busy everyday lives.

This may surprise people who have the idea that Americans are always showing affection. In general, it's probably true that we do tend to be more openly affectionate than Japanese. But what some people don't seem to realize is that what looks or sounds like affection is often just a simple greeting and sometimes only empty words.

Take "I love you" for example. It seems like a very clear, direct expression of love, but often it's not. In fact, in my opinion, this is one of the most overused expressions in the English language. A lot of people use it instead of saying "goodbye," often shortened to a simple "love you." This is especially common on the telephone, and it's used not only between lovers or family members, but also between friends. And in the language of lovers, it's often said with no real meaning behind it or just as a response to a partner saying it first. Even if one person really means it, the other may simply repeat the words with no meaning at all.

Amy Tan's novel *The Joy Luck Club* has such a scene: Suddenly, Lena feels a genuine surge of love for her husband. Reaching over, she "touched his hand and said, 'Harold, I love you.' And he looked in the rearview mirror, backing up the car, and said, 'I love you, too. Did you lock the door?'" Obviously, something is missing.

It's hard, even in your own language, to express feelings of love or affection in an authentic or appropriate way. Sometimes it feels safer or more comfortable in a second language, but that may be risky too. For example the word *akogareru* is often translated as "to long for something" in English. While it's fine to say that you "long to travel abroad," saying that you "long for a person" or you "long to be with someone" can only be used with a lover since it has a sexual meaning. In fact, I once received a letter with that expression from a happily married Japanese male friend. I knew that he really just meant "I miss you," or "I look forward to seeing you," but I still felt a little shocked.

I suppose how direct people are in expressing affection depends a lot on their own personality. Americans may generally be more direct than Japanese, but there are a lot of us who prefer a more indirect approach when it comes to the language of love. It's just too easy to forget the meaning behind the words if we use them too much. And that, for me, is what's nice about Valentine's Day. It's a yearly reminder that expressing love or affection is something we should do consciously, not as an empty daily habit. ∎

To Smoke or Not to Smoke

I grew up with parents who chain-smoked. I used to watch my mother breathe smoke deep into her lungs and think, "How crazy! I'll never do that." But by the age of 14, I was smoking too. Like all my friends, I smoked because I wasn't supposed to. It made us feel grown-up and free. When I spent the night with my best friend, Beth, we always climbed out on the roof from her second floor bedroom window and smoked cigarettes late at night beneath the stars. That was the coolest of the cool, we thought.

I stopped smoking around the age of 20 because I noticed I couldn't breathe very well when I rode my bicycle up and down hills. Besides, at 20 American kids are basically considered adults anyway, so I didn't need to rebel or prove I was grown up anymore. Quitting wasn't easy, but, lucky for me, I cared more about sports than cigarettes, so it was easier for me than for a lot of people. As a former smoker, I understand the charm of tobacco and the difficulty of giving it up. But, at the same time, I made a decision to quit, and I certainly don't want to breathe someone else's smoke now.

Of course, I have lots of company. Smoking has become controversial worldwide because of the dangers and unpleasantness of breathing secondhand smoke. Recent statistics show that around 3,700 Americans die every year from this so-called "passive smoke." And about 1,000 of those people are New Yorkers. That may help to explain why New York has the strictest anti-smoking laws in the US. In December of 2002, the mayor banned smoking in almost all public places, including restaurants, bars, and even in pool halls and bowling alleys. Most other states have their own restrictions against public smoking. While some people say this discriminates unfairly against smokers and others simply ignore the laws, enough Americans support the anti-smoking movement that it will probably continue to grow.

People love to see America as "the land of individuality and freedom," but on the issue of smoking, Japan fits this description better than the US. Granted, Japan is not the smoker's paradise it used to be. There are a growing number of smoke-free public places and more and more people who support this kind of ban. Laws are getting stricter here as well. But it's still almost impossible to go out at night and not sit next to or near a smoker. What's worse though, most smokers don't seem to care where their smoke is going. And usually it's going right into the face of the person sitting next to them.

Of course, some smokers are more considerate. Just the other day, at a favorite *izakaya* of mine, a man sitting at the same table asked me if it was ok to smoke. I answered honestly that I didn't mind, as long as the smoke went in the other direction. He and his date moved to the counter so he wouldn't have to worry about where his smoke went, but it was a little odd that he didn't ask the same question at the counter. Obviously, he only asked me because I wasn't Japanese, though the Japanese friend I was with feels exactly the same way I do about smoking.

Times have certainly changed. Back when I was a kid, the whole world was a smoker's paradise. The expressions "secondhand smoke" and "passive smoke" didn't exist, and nobody cared where you lit up. Nowadays "to smoke or not to smoke" may still be a personal choice, but smoking in public will never be quite so simple again. ∎

Sake and Other Things of the Heart

I love Japanese sake. So when I heard that an American woman who works at a brewery in Nagano was going to give a lecture in Tokyo, I was thrilled. Little did I know that I would get a lot more than just a lecture on sake from her.

I had read about Sarah Cummings before in the newspaper, so I knew who she was. Everyone knows the sake-brewing world is mainly a man's world, and a very traditional one, so any woman in that field stands out. And Sarah Cummings is not only a woman, but also an American, which makes her role as Managing Director of a sake brewery even more unusual. But, though her position is unusual, Cummings joins a growing group of Westerners in Japan who have a deep love and respect for certain aspects of Japanese culture and want to do their part to keep those things alive.

Cummings' lecture was hosted by an organization of mostly foreign businesspeople in Japan. Not being a businessperson myself, I had never attended such an event and wasn't sure what to expect. When I arrived, men in suits immediately started introducing themselves to me, and there was a lot of handshaking and exchanging of business cards. Clearly, for most people, it was a professional opportunity for networking and making connections. For me, it was simply a chance to meet Sarah Cummings and hear her speak, and I must say, I felt a little guilty taking all those cards.

Once the lecture started, I was pleasantly surprised. Sarah Cummings didn't talk much about business. Or sake, for that matter.

She spoke mostly about the community of Obuse where she lives, how she came to live and work there, and the ways she and her company are involved in that community. We even saw a video of Sarah and her dog running to work together through the early morning snow! Even though the setting for the lecture was a bit formal, Sarah Cummings didn't speak like a business professional or an elite specialist. In fact, she spoke more like "the girl next door," immediately likeable, unpretentious, and pure of heart. And she knew what she was talking about.

During the question-answer period, the business questions poured in. One woman wanted to know how Cummings managed to win consistent profits for her company since it had suffered losses before she took over management. Cummings talked around the question, not seeming to want to take credit for the company's success. A man from Australia then asked, very seriously and articulately, how to attract the tourist business in order to make more profits. Cummings answered simply: her company didn't worry about that much. They preferred to focus on their own community and how they could help make it better.

And that's what they do. Through all kinds of activities, like festivals and tours, they work hard to promote the region's history, arts, and culture, and they support the local artists and craftsmen/women who preserve those traditions as well. They also organize volunteer activities, like regular trash clean-up events, to keep the area beautiful. And, of course, they practice some of the old sake-making techniques, keeping those traditions alive and creating top-quality *jizake* the people of Obuse can be proud of.

Sarah Cummings has certainly been lucky to find these generous people and such a wonderful place for herself in Japan, and the community is also lucky to have found her. Her talk helped me to remember what is truly important, and it has much more to do with the heart than the pocketbook. ∎

Body Language

Sometimes the differences between Japanese and English make me laugh and sometimes they make me think, "Wow! Language really is culture." Just in language about the body, there's plenty to laugh and think about.

I have a friend who, like me, just started working as a translator. We often help each other out since her native language is Japanese and mine is English. Recently, she asked me about an expression in a romance novel, "His hands cupped her head." She couldn't picture a man cupping a woman's head in his hands. I thought the problem might be the word *cup* used as a verb, but it wasn't. She could easily imagine making your hands into the shape of a cup, for example, "Cup your hands and fill them with water." No, that wasn't the problem. The problem was the word *head*.

That's when we both discovered Japanese and American heads are not the same! I also remembered something I often hear friends at the gym say: "*Atama wo arau.*" This had always sounded odd to me, because an English speaker would never say, "I'm going to wash my head"; rather, we would say, "I'm going to wash my hair." In fact, the image of washing your head is pretty funny. The *head*, in English, generally includes everything above the neck. Another English expression makes this clear: "She has a good head on her shoulders," which suggests a person who is intelligent in a practical kind of way. Once my friend understood "head" means the round ball above a person's shoulders, she had no trouble picturing a man cupping a woman's head in his hands.

Then there's *ashi*. It seems unfair to me that legs and feet have to share this word in Japanese, while in English they have their own separate identities. Of course feet and legs can't complain, but when I use *ashi* to mean "foot," I always feel like I'm doing some kind of injustice to legs, and vice versa.

My favorites, though, are words that reveal something about culture. I often sense from language that Japanese people have a more positive image of the body than Westerners. The word *hana-mizu*, for example, sounds so much cleaner and more natural than the rather unpleasant English equivalent, *snot*. And *oppai* versus *breast* reveals something similar. Even though my family was not religious, I, like most Americans, grew up with the Christian sense that the body is shameful in some way. That's probably why every English word for *breast* has a fairly strong sexual connotation. We do have the expression *breast-feeding* for mothers, but many people prefer the euphemism, *nursing*. It simply doesn't feel that comfortable to say the word *breast* aloud. *Oppai*, on the other hand, is a word everyone seems to feel comfortable with.

An English friend who's married to a Japanese man told me a funny story about this. At a public bath in Japan, her two small children reached for her breasts, singing out happily, "*Oppai, oppai!*" as if it were a game. This scene is unimaginable in either the UK or the US where there isn't even an appropriate word in children's language for *breast*, and, besides, children who tried playing such a game would surely be scolded. Personally, I find the Japanese way of thinking healthy and refreshing compared to the rather repressed Western way.

We can learn a lot about culture from all kinds of words, or we can just be entertained by them. Either way, it's certainly true that words speak volumes. ∎

The Chopsticks Debate

The other day I was eating alone at a revolving sushi (*kaiten zushi*) place. A very nice man sitting next to me started a conversation by complimenting my ability to use chopsticks. We quickly moved on to the next topic, but I was reminded of a very heated discussion that came up recently on one of the mailing lists I subscribe to. It was about chopsticks, and, for many Westerners in Japan, that "dreaded" compliment.

Now why do some foreigners get so upset when Japanese people tell them they use chopsticks well? I discovered several answers to this question as I followed the chopsticks debate on my mailing list.

Perhaps the main reason is that for anyone who has lived in Japan for awhile, say more than a year, using chopsticks is no big deal. There's nothing hard about it, so it seems strange to be complimented on what anyone, with a little practice, could do. One person even wrote that being complimented on the ability to use chopsticks is like being complimented on the ability to walk. And that's why some people are insulted by it.

There's probably a cultural perception gap here. For Japanese, there is clearly a wrong way and a right way to use chopsticks, and I often hear the complaint that even young Japanese don't know the right way. That's probably why many Japanese, with their high standards, don't see using chopsticks as so simple. On the other hand, most Westerners who live in Japan use chopsticks comfortably every day and don't really think about whether they're doing it right or wrong.

The second reason is a more psychological one. For some Westerners, the comment, "Oh, you use chopsticks so well!" means this: "We're Japanese and you're not, so no one expects you to be able to use chopsticks." In other words, this compliment makes a lot of foreigners feel like outsiders, when, in fact, they really just want to be treated like everyone else at the table. This may seem like paranoia or a case of taking things too seriously. But the fact is, a lot of foreigners who have made their home in Japan are quite sensitive about being seen as outsiders.

I have to admit, I myself have had both of these reactions at one time or another on hearing this compliment. But I found a new way of looking at the whole thing through the mailing list debate. One person wrote in suggesting that this compliment is simply a social ritual. It doesn't mean anything really; rather, for a lot of Japanese, it's just a way to break the ice and start a conversation, a kind of *aisatsu*.

This seems right to me now. And it's clear that's exactly what was going on the other day at the *kaiten zushi* place. The chopsticks compliment was just a simple greeting for starting a conversation.

The funny thing is I'd much rather use chopsticks than a knife and fork. The reason? Well, I grew up eating American style, but most Japanese eat European style. There's a big difference in the way the knife and fork are used, and some people would say the European style is more sophisticated. When I go out for a formal dinner in Japan, for example to a French restaurant or a wedding, not only do I forget which fork I'm supposed to use, but I'm also the only person at the table switching my fork back and forth between hands as I cut the meat. Sounds silly, I know, but I always feel awkward in these situations. Give me an *izakaya* and nice, simple chopsticks any day! ■

In Praise of Japanese Men

In the early 1980's, Donald Keene wrote a very interesting essay called "Japanese Men" which, although more than 20 years old now, still rings true. One of his main points is that while Japanese women tend to have a very positive image in the West, Japanese men are often stereotyped as workaholics or simply ignored. It's true. Japanese men are not seen very often in American movies, books, or the media for example, and when they are, they tend to be shown in unattractive roles. Anyone who lives in Japan knows that these images are unfair, but for some reason the attractiveness of Japanese men has not been exported to

America and other Western countries very successfully.

Even so, a lot of Western women living in Japan find Japanese men extremely attractive. "Attractiveness" includes looks of course, but that's not all there is to it. For some Western women, including myself, one of the most attractive qualities of Japanese men is their communication style, a style very different from that of most American men. Communication is often the key to a good relationship, whether it's friendship, romance, or marriage. And, in general, Japanese men are easy to talk to. Here's why.

Japanese men are good listeners. They tend to listen quietly, giving encouraging signals (*aizuchi*), and they wait until the other person finishes speaking before they start talking. Of course this is Japanese style, not only men's style. When I talk to someone who listens this way, I feel like they really want to hear what I have to say. And this is what most women want: Someone who truly listens.

I suppose there's nothing so hard about listening well if the topic is simple. But when the conversation becomes a discussion, and especially when people have different opinions, the art of listening becomes more difficult. Still, I find that most Japanese men continue to listen well, without interrupting, even in a more emotional discussion. They seem able to accept opinions that are different from their own, without feeling threatened. So my second point is that Japanese men are easy to disagree with. In other words, it's possible to agree to disagree with no bad feelings.

And American men? Well, in my experience, American men in general are much harder to communicate with, especially when there are different opinions. This is probably because they're taught to have strong opinions and to win arguments. Showing that you're right and the other person is wrong is a very common discussion style among American men. This kind of "conversation" is more like an argument, with lots of interrupting. A lot of Americans, even some women, like this style.

I've never liked the argument style of conversation myself, even when I lived in America. Some people find it exciting and intellectually stimulating, but others, like me, just find it stressful. I'll never forget one time when an old boyfriend and I went to a movie together. He loved it and I didn't. Simple enough, right? But he went on and on trying to prove he was right and I was wrong about the movie. We ended up mad at each other when it would have been so much easier just to accept that we had different opinions.

It's this kind of difference in cultural styles that makes some Americans feel that Japan is a more gentle culture than America. Obviously, not all men fit these descriptions, but it is this kind of gentleness in Japanese men that so many Western women find attractive. I just wish more Americans had the opportunity to experience it. ∎

The Kindness of Strangers

It's early morning and here I am again, packed on a rush-hour train with all the other people going to work or school. The train stops at Tokyo's Shibuya Station, and we're all crushed in the push to get off. Everyone looks sleepy and miserable. Finally, I get to the Yamanote line ticket gate, and suddenly cheerful voices are calling out, "Good morning! Good morning!" It sounds like they really mean it, like they know exactly how we feel and are trying their best to cheer us up. And it works! They may just be doing their job, but that simple kindness brings unexpected pleasure. In fact, I'm often surprised by how the smallest acts of kindness can brighten up the day and sometimes make a big difference.

That's definitely how I felt one cold, rainy day last spring. Have you ever noticed that it always rains when you have an important meeting? I was walking to a job interview late in the afternoon. The rain was starting to make my hair frizzy and my clothes damp. On top of that, I had missed lunch and was beginning to feel pretty grumpy. I couldn't go to an interview feeling like that.

I knew I had to eat something, but there wasn't much time and there was only one place open nearby, a tiny coffee shop. I walked in and found myself to be the only customer. And lunch was already over. "Couldn't I get a sandwich?" I asked, a little desperation in my voice. The waitress hesitated and said they could only make pancakes at that hour. Hmmm. Pancakes were better than nothing, I thought, and said OK. I heard low voices as she talked to the cook in the kitchen. Then she came back out and said they could heat up some rolled cabbage and make toast. "That's all we have," she apologized sincerely. But to me, a hot lunch of rolled cabbage and toast sounded like heaven. And it was! That was one of the most delicious meals I've ever eaten. To this day, I'm sure I got the job I interviewed for because of the kindness of those people.

I suppose most people expect kindness from their friends, but when even strangers do something special for us, something they don't have to do, it seems like the world is a pretty good place to be. Japanese friends and acquaintances often tell me how much they appreciate the kindness of strangers when they visit the US. And that reminds me of something that surprised me when I made a trip home. In some shops in Texas, there's a bowl of pennies by the cash register. When you pay the bill, you can use those pennies if you need them. Sometimes the store clerk will even take a penny out of his or her own pocket and give it to you if you don't have one. Of course, a penny is no big deal, but that small consideration always gives me a good feeling.

Most people probably don't even realize that the small things they do at work make a big difference to the people they do them for. Just being cheerful and friendly or bending the rules a little to help someone out may have more of an impact than you ever imagined. I'm often tempted to thank the guys at the station for encouraging me with their bright morning greetings, or go by and tell those people at the coffee shop how I'll always remember that hot, rolled cabbage lunch. There's no doubt about it, a little kindness goes a long way. ∎

Photograph by Tadamitsu Nakagawa

Kay Hetherly was born in Austin, Texas, and grew up in Houston. After finishing an MA program in English and American Literature at the University of Wisconsin, Madison, she moved to Tokyo where she has been teaching American literature and culture since 1991. She also works as a translator. From 1996-1998, Kay was a regular guest on NHK's radio English conversation program, and continues to write monthly essays for that program's text. The first collection of those essays, called *American Pie*, was put out by NHK Publishing in 2000. She has also published articles on various writers, including Charles Dickens, Alice Walker, Amy Tan, and Abe Kobo. Kay enjoys her Tokyo life, especially when she's playing squash or drinking *nihonshu* with her squash buddies.

デザイン：畑中猛
イラストレーション：にしごりるみ
校正：筧万理子

Kitchen Table Talk
~Anything and Everything Essays on America and Japan~

2003年11月15日　第1刷発行
2020年４月５日　第20刷発行

著者　　ケイ・ヘザリ
　　　　©2003 Kay Hetherly
発行者　森永公紀
発行所　NHK出版
　　　　〒150-8081 東京都渋谷区宇田川町41-1
　　　　電話 0570-002-046（編集）
　　　　　　 0570-000-321（注文）
　　　　ホームページ　http://www.nhk-book.co.jp
　　　　振替 00110-1-49701
印刷・製本　大日本印刷

定価はカバーに表示してあります。
落丁・乱丁本はお取替えいたします。

本書の無断複写（コピー）は、著作権法で認められた
場合を除き、著作権侵害となります。

Printed in Japan
ISBN 978-4-14-035063-8 C0082